Accession no.
01086882

WITHDRAWN

TRACEY MOFFATT

LIBRARY
Tel: 01244 375444   Ext: 3301

This book is to be returned on or before the
last date stamped below. Overdue charges
will be incurred by the late return of books.

Chester
A College of the
University of Liverpool

UCO LIBRARY
13 MAY 2002

UCO LIBRARY
15 JUN 2002

- 5 FEB 2003

29 OCT 2003

2 6 JAN 2004

1 8 MAY 2007

13 MAY 2004

1 1 FEB 2005

- 8 MAR 2005

CANCELLED

- 6 JUN 2005

05 JU

1 3 DEC

0 5 MAR 2007

2 9 FEB 2008

D1514255

TRACEY MOFFATT

EDITOR/CURATOR MICHAEL SNELLING

AN IMA/ASIALINK PROJECT
BRISBANE 1999

1390776

CHESTER COLLEGE

ACC. No.
01086882

DEPT.

CLASS No.
779·092 mo7

LIBRARY

© Copyright the authors and the Institute of Modern Art, Brisbane, 1999. All rights reserved. No part of this publication may be reproduced, stored in a retrieval system, transmitted or utilised in any form or by any means, electronic, mechanical, photocopying, recording or otherwise, without permission in writing from the publishers.

Published and produced by the Institute of Modern Art
Managing Editor: Michael Snelling
Editorial/production assistance: David Broker, Anna Marsden, Ruth McDougall, Laurel Davis, Kate Mathers, Holly Arden
Design: Ric Aqui

Pre-press: Colour Chiefs, Fortitude Valley
Printed in Brisbane by InPrint

National Library of Australia Cataloguing-in-Publication data:

Moffatt, Tracey.
Tracey Moffatt.

ISBN 1 875792 29 5.

1. Moffatt, Tracey. 2. Photography, Artistic. 3. Video art.
I. Snelling, Michael. II. Institute of Modern Art (Brisbane, Qld.).
III. Asialink (Melbourne, Vic.). IV. Title.

702.81

INSTITUTE OF MODERN ART

608 Ann Street, Fortitude Valley, Brisbane Q 4006
GPO Box 1897, Brisbane Q 4001 Australia
Tel: +61 7 3252 5750 Fax: +61 7 3252 5072
im@ima.org.au www.ima.org.au

ASIALINK

11–13 Lincoln Square South
Carlton VIC 3053
Melbourne Australia
Tel: +61 3 9349 1899 Fax: +61 3 9347 1768

ACKNOWLEDGEMENTS

PAGES 15–57: The photograhic series *Laudanum*, *Up in the Sky*, *Scarred for Life*, courtesy of Roslyn Oxley9 Gallery, Sydney (tel: +61 2 9331 1919).

PAGES 58–63: The video and films *Heaven*, *beDevil* and *Night Cries: A Rural Tragedy*, courtesy of Ronin Films, Canberra, for distribution in Australia/New Zealand (tel: +61 2 6248 0851). *beDevil* is distributed outside Australia/New Zealand by Southern Star Distribution, Sydney (tel: +61 2 9202 8555).

PAGE 64: Stills from the documentary film by Jane Cole, *Up in the Sky: Tracey Moffatt in New York*, 1999, courtesy of Ronin Films, Canberra, and Jane Cole.

Permission to use the essay 'Specific Climates' by Régis Durand was generously provided by Fundacío 'la Caxia', Barcelona, Spain, and Régis Durand. The original text appeared in *Tracey Moffatt*, published in 1999 by Fundacío 'la Caxia'. Régis Durand is director of the Centre National de la Photographie de Paris.

Permission to use the interview by Gerald Matt with Tracey Moffatt was generously provided by Cantz. The original interview appeared in *Tracey Moffatt*, published in 1998 by Cantz Verlag, Stuttgart, Germany.

Invaluable, even inestimable, assistance was also provided by Roslyn Oxley, Russell Storer and Luke Roberts.

Thanks, as always, to Suhanya Raffel.

Alison Carroll, manager of arts programs at Asialink, has provided unwavering support with her usual clear-sighted vision.

Finally, a very big thanks to Tracey Moffatt who responded at short notice with enthusiasm.   —M.S.

REPRODUCTION NOTES

COVER, PAGES 2 & 6: Details from the photographic series *Laudanum* are reproduced as duotone (cover) and monotone (pages 2 & 6). PAGES 59, 61 & 63: Stills from *Heaven*, *beDevil* & *Night Cries* are reproduced from video.

TRACEY MOFFATT

The Institute of Modern Art in Brisbane and the Asialink Centre at the University of Melbourne are honoured to present the work of Tracey Moffatt.

This book encompasses the decade from 1989 to 1999, presenting in all, seven works; three films and four series of stills. In Brisbane, the exhibition comprised the films *Night Cries: A Rural Tragedy* (1989), *beDevil* (1993), and *Heaven* (1998) and the photographic series *Scarred for Life* (1994), *Up in the Sky* (1997) and *Laudanum* (1998).

After its premiere at the IMA, the tour in Asia includes the 1989 work *Something More* and subtracts *Laudanum* and *Heaven*.

The IMA gratefully acknowledges the support of our major sponsor Arts Queensland. The IMA and Asialink gratefully acknowledge the generous support of the Australia Council, the Australian government's arts funding and advisory body and the Department of Foreign Affairs and Trade in presenting this exhibition.

Institute of Modern Art
Brisbane, Australia
8 September – 9 October 1999

The series *Something More* is from the collection of the Museum of Contemporary Art, Sydney (purchased with assistance from the Thea Proctor Memorial Fund, 1992); *Scarred for Life* and *Up in the Sky* are courtesy of the artist and Roslyn Oxley9 Gallery, Sydney; and the images from *Laudanum* are courtesy of Reg Richardson, Sydney. *Night Cries: A Rural Tragedy; beDevil; Heaven;* and *Up in the Sky: Tracey Moffatt in New York*, are distributed by Ronin Films, Canberra. The organisers thank the lenders for supporting this tour.

FOREWORD

The University of Melbourne is an international university. It is committed to encouraging international values, perspectives and experience. This includes working energetically with others who are committed to developing cultural understanding between the peoples of our region.

Tracey Moffatt is a young Australian artist of growing international reputation. Her work crosses cultures and physical media in a dynamic, witty, engrossing, and often confronting way.

The University of Melbourne, through our own Asialink Centre, is delighted to work in partnership with
—the Australia Council, the Australian Government's arts advisory and funding body,
—the Australian Department of Foreign Affairs and Trade, through the Australia Korea Foundation and the Australia China Council,
—the Institute of Modern Art in Brisbane,
—the Roslyn Oxley9 Gallery in Sydney,
—Artsonje in Korea and
—the Taipei Fine Arts Museum
to realise this first solo exhibition of Tracey Moffatt's work in the Asian region.

I trust you will enjoy the exhibition.

Roger Peacock
Vice President, University Development
The University of Melbourne

Artsonje Center
Seoul, Korea
23 February – 15 April 2001

Artsonje Museum
Kyongju, Korea
27 April – 1 July 2001

Taipei Fine Arts Museum
Taipei, Taiwan
11 August – 23 September 2001

CONTENTS

8

INTRODUCTION
by Michael Snelling

10

SPECIFIC CLIMATES
by Régis Durand

15

PHOTOGRAPHS, FILM & VIDEO
Laudanum, 1998
Up in the Sky, 1997
Scarred for Life, 1994
Something More, 1989
Heaven, 1997
beDevil, 1993
Night Cries: A Rural Tragedy, 1990

64

AN INTERVIEW WITH TRACEY MOFFATT
by Gerald Matt

69

BIOGRAPHY & BIBLIOGRAPHY

INTRODUCTION

BY

MICHAEL SNELLING

'An Australian friend encouraged me to do a Sri Lankan reading of *Night Cries*. What would a Sri Lankan reading be? Wrong question, you can't know what it is until you do it, because a reading is in part deciphering and in part invention in the sense of making connections.'[1]

— Laleen Jayamanne, 1992

1 Laleen Jayamanne, 'Love me tender, love me true, never let me go—A Sri Lankan reading of Tracey Moffatt's *Night Cries*', in: Sneja Gunew, Anna Yeatman, (eds), *Feminism and the politics of difference*, Allen and Unwin, Sydney, 1993, p. 73

One of the most striking characteristics of Tracey Moffatt's practice is the multiplicity of readings and uncertainty of resolution that the work provokes. In her photography she manages to suggest both the familiar and the singular by using elements of the documentary with the constructed, the still single image with the series, a kind of jump cut narrative that forfeits closure and a refusal to nominate a single meaning for the work. In her films and videos, except for *Heaven*, she introduces the obvious artifice of the stage, and a deliberate framing more akin to a series of moving stills than a conventional film. By frequently citing inspirations as diverse as Pasolini, American Roller Derby, surfies dropping their daks, Japanese and Australian cinema and her own subconscious, she provides clues to her own intentions.

Moffatt has a love of, and pays homage to, an eclectic collection of styles that she combines with a desire to experiment by mixing and matching language and convention. There is an invigorating casual challenge in her interweaving of film, photography and stage that brings much energy to the over exploited and sometimes slightly exhausted media of film and photography. The dynamism of European and American documentary photography in the 40s, 50s and 60s, and the beautiful gritty black and white Italian films of the sixties are recognisable in the look and feel of *Scarred for Life* and *Up in the Sky*.

In this documentary tradition there lies a certain active subservience, a willingness, in theory at least, to sink into the background, to watch with clarity. The photographer takes a directorial up-front role when working in non-documentary capacities, such as commercial or fashion photography. Tracey Moffatt works in the manner of a film or theatre director constructing realities that look like documents but which she often refers to as fantasies.

In *Something More* the lush artifice, saturated colour and metallic sheen of cibachrome counterpoints black and white images that combine in a story of thwarted aspirations and failed dreams. The most straightforward reading of the series of nine images is of a young beautiful woman seeking to break away from her rural setting to reach the big city and in the attempt meeting violence and an ignominious end sprawled face down and violated across the thin white line of her highway to freedom. While this is familiar territory as far as a story goes, Moffatt brings her own slant to the scenario. Race, class and gender all complicate the predictability of the narrative. When combined with the structural device of providing only snippets of the story, *Something More* moves from predictable misfortune to miserable desolation.

Night Cries: A Rural Tragedy tills similar soil in a bigger paddock, this time built around the love/hate relationship of an ailing aging mother and frustrated carer daughter. The main elements include a white mother and a black daughter, a mise en scène that reminds one of an Albert Namatjira/Robert Wilson painted set and a pendulous emotional balance that gently exposes the ambivalent commitments of parent child relations. There is no spoken word between the two protagonists, instead a soundscape that provides a backbeat to the unfolding drama. However it is the inescapably ironic presence of the sweetly toned country singer Jimmy Little, who first sings his hit song Royal Telephone, and then silently mimes Love Me Tender, that undermines the already fragile cliché of the story line. When one adds to the mix the forced adoption practices of Australian government assimilation policy, the mother/daughter melodrama turns tragic.

beDevil is a 90-minute film containing three, for want of a better description, ghost stories. All are designed to suggest the proscenium and, as with *Night Cries*, often filmed with the still image lurking at the beginning or end of the moving camera. *beDevil* is even more ambiguous than the earlier work. It clearly positions the three small vignettes of communities as micro-stories within a larger narrative of ethnicity, gender, place and spiritual and cultural beliefs.

The series *Laudanum* is set in a claustrophobic English Victorian interior, apparently drawing its inspiration from a mélange of trashy fiction, German expressionist film, erotic and vampiric literature and a pictorial style of photography. Two women, a white mistress and an Asian maid, enact some sort of story that, while suggesting all the influences cited above, manages to suggest much more than it discloses. What are these two up to? Is this a simple story of colonial/class repression? Are the women lovers or is there a nonconsensual violence being perpetrated by the mistress upon the maid? All that and more.

There is an ever-increasing truckload of writing about Moffatt's work. Much of it seeks to penetrate the ambiguity of her scenarios. In doing so this writing explores a raft of possibilities this title cannot accommodate including the positioning of indigenous Australians as protagonists and the blend of realism and fantasy. There is a particular relationship to the 'place' of Australia that is represented in most of her work (*Pet Thang* and *Guapa* are two exceptions, located in the ether of the studio).

The complexity of conception is, for me, one of the great pleasures in engaging with Moffatt's work. By working with the potent mix of gender, class, race and colonialism, with a broad palette of influences from popular culture to high art, presented through the most popular media of the 20th century, and always depicted against expectation, she manages to build an ongoing tension that repays repeated engagement.

SPECIFIC CLIMATES

BY

RÉGIS DURAND

Whether filmic or photographic, each of Tracey Moffatt's images is carefully constructed. None of them presents itself as a 'reproduction of reality'; on the contrary, they are produced by meticulous artistry in the studio or in artificial decors, after a preparatory phase of drawing and the creation of a veritable storyboard, as well as a casting process and a technical study.

Many artists work in this way today—among the more well-known, one may think of Jeff Wall or Cindy Sherman (with a somewhat more intimate, artisanal character for the latter's productions). What is particular in Tracey Moffatt's work, among other things, is her way of not only shifting from film to photography or from photography to film, but continually crisscrossing the two. In fact, one must consider that for her they form but a single practice, modulated from one project to the next. This modulation is not a simple alternance, for each of the two practices exercises considerable pressure on the other: cinema upsetting photography's character as an image closed in on itself: photography cutting against the grain of cinema's 'natural' temporality and production of narrative. One can see that this back-and-forth movement is a dual way of approaching a heterogeneous and unstable contemporary reality, a reality that feeds on the inexhaustible flux of images conveyed and recycled by the world's televisions, and also on individual memories and fantasies. Identifiable references emerge from all this, specific climates if you will, whether geographic, social or psychic. In other words, Tracey Moffatt's work appears as a surprising mix of the indeterminate and the brutally precise, the timeless and the contemporary. The result is a taut, sometimes disturbing body of work. The following remarks aim to bring out some of its points of tension and to identify a few of their implications.

OPEN IMAGES, CLOSED IMAGES

It is sometimes said that photography is a 'closed' image, more closed in any case than painting, to the extent that its link to the referent remains strong, even when it is enigmatic. And how much more closed than cinema, among whose particularities is that of 'opening universes' by introducing time into the images.[1] In Tracey Moffatt's work, the fixed image and the filmic image ceaselessly tend toward each other. The fixed image seems to be a 'freeze frame' plucked from the unfolding of a film—an impression reinforced by the fact that it never exists in an isolated state, but always within a group, a series, which seems to point

1 For this point see Jean Louis Schefer, *Du monde et du mouvement des images*, Cahiers du cinema, Collection Essais, Paris, 1997

toward a possible narrative content, or at least an intention, an energy turned in that direction. A sketchy content, to be sure, but powerfully present, to the point of creating the feeling that the fixed images belong to some vanished film. As to the films themselves, their diegesic energy sometimes seems to be carried forward by the sound as much as the images, which are on the verge of freezing into 'tableaux'.

However, these two contrary movements should not be cause for illusion: each of the genres retains its own dynamic and its inherent laws. The themes and decors may be closely related, but they nonetheless remain separated by the mode of realisation; the random, fragmented reading of the photographs, the irreversible temporal constraint of the films. From this point of view, one may consider the photographic works as having a more open character than the films, to the extent that they leave a greater share of invention to the spectator.

STYLES AND CLIMATES OF IMAGES

Tracey Moffatt's images, as we have mentioned, often have an enigmatic character. In the photographic series in particular, what is at stake is not always immediately perceptible. In *Something More*, for example, there seems to be an attempt to tell a 'story', but due to the framing and the blurring of certain images it remains sketchy and uncertain. In *Pet Thang*, the juxtaposition of the woman's body and the toy plays on the dreamlike, fantasmatic character of the associations: a block of images, not an organised, orientated sequence. In the series *Guapa*, on the contrary, each image of these women engaged in roller-skate elimination trials seems to be excerpted from a continuum—a competition, a 'film' of the events—to which we do not have access. Similarly, in *Up in the Sky*, each shot refers to so many possible stories; something has happened, or is about to happen.

Now, when there is an enigma of meaning, when the scene is not immediately convertible and remains unresolved, two elements spring to the foreground of our reading: the materiality of what is shown, its referent in the world; and the style or styles. In Tracey Moffatt's work, the referential content is at once present and absent. Absent, because these images are clearly fabricated and do not claim to reflect any exterior reality. But present, because they nonetheless evoke certain precise situations: a geography, for example, the Australian outback in *Up in the Sky* and *Night Cries*; or sporting competitions, as in *Guapa*. But their true referent is Imaginary. It is our memory of other images that have reached us from cinema, television, photography albums, or—not the least important source—from dreams and their hybrid productions. Thus it is a matter of mediatised 'reality', deformed and 'fictionalised'—a reality thoroughly worked over by narrative and iconographic styles (the aesthetic of late neorealist film, that of Pasolini in *Accatone*, for example, or a certain form of exotic romance in vogue in the 50s and 60s). In fact, the referent and the style(s) are one in the work of Tracey Moffatt.

'THE TERROR OF UNCERTAIN SIGNS'

In a well-known passage, Roland Barthes produced a remarkable condensation of the question of meaning and its reading, as it could be formulated in an epoch which sought to describe the plurality of the 'open work' and the spectator's role as 'producer'; 'Every image is polysemous; it implies, subjacent to its signifiers, a 'floating chain' of signifieds of which the reader can select some and ignore the rest. Polysemy gives rise to a questioning of meaning, and this questioning always appears as a dysfunction ... Hence, in every society a

2 Roland Barthes, 'Rhetoric of the image' in *The responsibility of forms*, Hill and Wang, New York, 1985, p. 28, (translated from the French by Richard Howard)

certain number of techniques are developed in order to fix the floating chain of signifieds, to combat the terror of uncertain signs, the linguistic message is one of these techniques.'[2]

Tracey Moffatt's images are, as we have seen, deliberately polysemeous, and it is precisely this 'floating chain' of signifiers that constitutes their strangeness and wealth. Indeed, one of the characteristics of today's art, which distinguishes it from the popular iconographic sources upon which it so often draws (film, television, advertising etc.), is to increase this indeterminacy, against the attempts at reduction and fixation imposed by the social demand. In Tracey Moffatt's work the 'terror of uncertain signs' plays not only on the register of narrative or semantic indeterminacy, but also on the diffuse sentiment of a parallel world, outside social and moral norms. This is the 'Gothic' side of her work, the disquieting atmospheres and the decors, the obscure impression of menacing forces. The film *beDevil* is composed of three 'ghost stories'; and in the recent photographic series *Laudanum*, reveries or visions supposedly produced by the tincture of opium that gives the series its name are blended with a vague ambience of 'colonial decadence', in whose depths bloom all sorts of fantasies. The decors which are an essential element of the 'Gothic' in both its literary and filmic versions, are always carefully calculated to evoke a particular atmosphere, but one that is vague enough to leave room for all individual projections. The 'uncanniness' that reigns in these works thus stems primarily from the fact that the signs float in a dimension which is close to that of dreams or waking reverie. And when text intervenes as an integral part of the works, for example in *Scarred for Life*, it is not in order to 'fix' anything at all, but to divert the caption from its rational function of anchoring—the function which Barthes, following Benjamin and Brecht, was thinking of in the remarks quoted above, and which the photographic doxa long held to be indispensable for the comprehension of the image. In Tracey Moffatt's work the caption only appears as such in *Scarred for Life*, where it serves to turn childhood scenes into traumatic memories. Far from fixing the meaning, this text-image mix gives rise to blocks charged with narrative and psychic energy (as in Freud's famous text, 'A child is being beaten').

In the other series, to the contrary, the text is seemingly anterior, underlying the final work. It exists as a scenario in a broad sense, that is, not only as a storyboard, but also as a universe of reference, a general 'climate', Thus, the text, while not present in the work as such, acts as a shifter of memories and allusions. *Laudanum*, for example, refers to an imaginary which one might qualify as 'Victorian Erotic'. Towards the middle of Queen Victoria's reign in England, the rigid social and moral conventions, which had not evolved at the same rate as the real social transformations, enforced an extremely strong repression of everything explicitly sexual, producing an equally powerful return of the repressed, notably in the form of an abundant erotic literature. This is also the close of a period of great colonial expansion, which fed all kinds of fantasies, mingling the desire for adventure, the myth of 'savagery' and racial difference, the fascination for the master-slave relation and so on. Thus one realises that numerous subtexts are present in this series, not the least of which is the evocation of the postcolonial situation (Australia, in this case), which many contemporary artists have explored.

HOW AUSTRALIAN IS IT?

In *How German is it—Wie Deutsch ist es* (1979), Walter Abish realises an indirect portrait of contemporary Germany by placing himself at once inside and outside the society, via characters, situations, manners of speaking, and allusions to the past, which he scrutinises with the detachment of an entomologist. Like most artists of her generation, Tracey Moffatt feels the greatest mistrust towards the reductive character of national identity, particularly where her own work is concerned. As we know, contemporary art is international, even if this postulate cannot help but raise many questions, particularly when it seems to perfectly match the discourse of economic globalisation. Tracey Moffatt, who now lives in New York, has taken certain distances from her country of origin, and understandably resists biographical interpretations of her work, with their unavoidable limitations.

This question of origins is nonetheless very present in her art, not as an explanatory principle that would effectively be reductive, but as one of the powerful energies that runs through it. First of all there is the literal question of origin, a delicate question if ever there was. Of Aboriginal birth before being confided to adoptive white parents, Tracey Moffatt is originally from the country, by opposition to those who colonised it. And this theme runs throughout her work in various forms, in the ambivalence of situations mixing scorn, resentment and guilt, where repression and explosions of emotion alternate. Because this question of origins forms part of her history, Tracey Moffatt is capable of another gaze upon herself, and capable of using that gaze as a vehicle and a metaphor for all kinds of questions. As an Australian, she knows how to use the extremely powerful stock of images that only such a country can produce—the solitude of the outback, the beauty and boredom of the desert, the mix of poverty and intensity that isolation produces in human relations, the almost experimental novelty of a country at once highly ancient and very new, with an extraordinary blend of races and cultures. Thus the origin is clearly irreducible to biographical facts. It is a personal myth, a fable that everyone ceaselessly writes and rewrites. It is this desire for origin, this inexhaustible source of fantasies and fictions, that ultimately matters, more than the actual origin.

DEVOURING TIME

Fictions 'clothe' our fantasies, distracting our attention from all that is too raw and brutal in them. One of Tracey Moffatt's strengths is to let us perceive something of these harsher energies, behind a very sophisticated construction. One of the most remarkable things in her work is the condensation between the various temporal strata brought into play by memories, dreams and fantasies, between which she shifts back and forth with no respect for chronology. The work is anachronous, floating between memories of different times and natures; memories of lived experience, whether physical or cultural (memories of places, films and music which have meant something to her); collective memories which overdetermine social relations in any given situation; imaginary memories of invented or appropriated identities. Why is it that this universe with its floating chronology, bearing rather few contemporary markers, is nonetheless perceived as absolutely contemporary, and not as a series of period pieces? It is because it matches movements that run through contemporary reality; the more-or-less distanced or ironic returns to older attitudes and aesthetics, an apparent confusion that is governed in reality by precise scenarios where atopia and anachronism alternate with violent reterritorialisation. By their frank artificiality, by the blend of fiction and uncoded indications, her works point up the different components of a fluctuating contemporary reality, which itself in a sense exists nowhere, if not in our continual attempts at its (re)construction. Here, the fully controlled scenarios and production techniques guarantee the creation of a truth-effect that few ethnographic-type documentaries are able to produce (for they are uneasy before the ineluctable necessity of a reflection on the laws of the medium, of the kind the great documentarists have always engaged in).

When Tracey Moffatt says that her subject is the staging of an 'urban Aboriginal culture', she defines a field of investigation, but also creates a very rich metaphor of the contemporary situation—a world of wandering and relocation, a world of hybridity and crossing signals, a floating world with so many images and stereotypes that it seems unreal, even while it is charged with very real and sometimes violent experiences. The figure of the 'Aboriginal', fascinating and hated when seen as the bearer of a knowledge of origins, is in its turn taken up into this great drift, becoming a symbol of the confused struggles with which we are now confronted.

IMAGES IN A CERTAIN ORDER ARRANGED

I have spoken of enigma. But the enigma implies something hidden, in Tracey Moffatt's work, as indeed in many supposedly enigmatic situations or representations, one must nonetheless accept the idea that everything is there, visible. Where, there? In the individual images, in the relations between them (in the series), but also in the readings we give of them. Before these images what we discover is not so much of the order of meaning, as of a somewhat hallucinated perception of several parallel times and universes. In the films, the narration (or at least a certain continuity) facilitates the illusion and momentary belief in these fragments of a 'fictive reality'. Because they are discontinuous, the photographic series render belief more difficult. But this very discontinuity constantly stimulates our curiosity. Identification and projection come relatively little into play; rather, there is the perception that something has taken form (or is about to take from), before which we are relatively ill-assured, conscious of this uncertainty and of the moment in which we experience it, the present time which slips away. It is the reverse, if you like, of what Roland Barthes and others after him saw in photography: not the image of something that has been, haloed with a wealth of temporal layers, but a surface cold like a mirror, referring whoever looks at it back to the historical present. This present, by definition, destroys and reconstitutes itself ceaselessly, even while we inquire into that which is there before us. And it is also of this fragile mobility that Tracey Moffatt speaks.

PHOTOGRAPHS, FILM & VIDEO

LAUDANUM

1998

Series of 19 photogravure prints on rag paper
76 × 57 cm (paper size), edition of 60

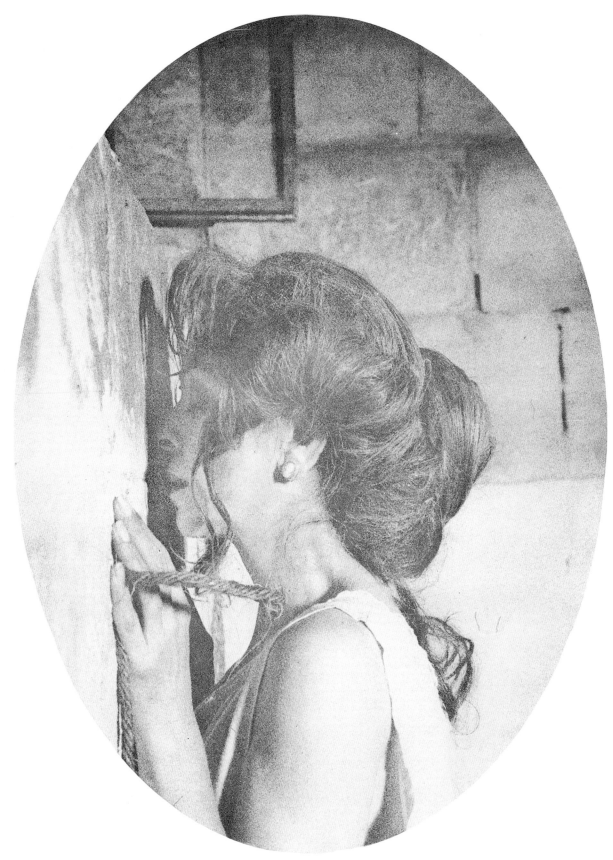

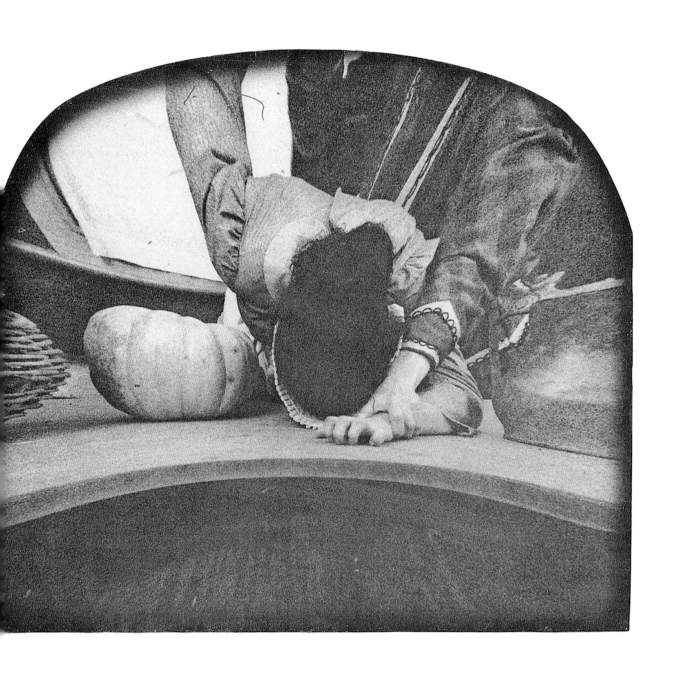

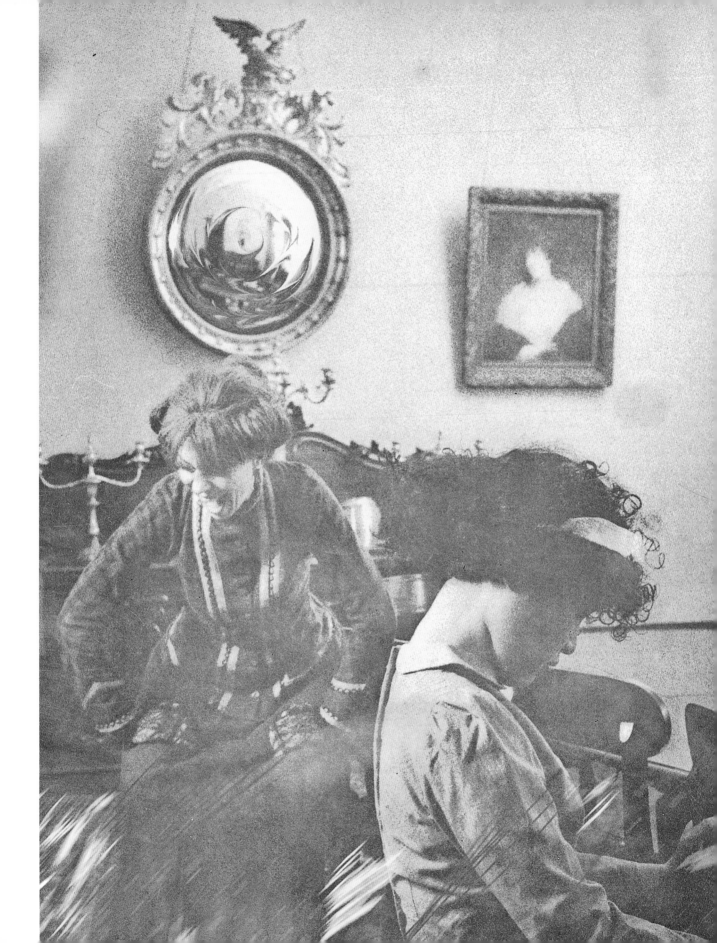

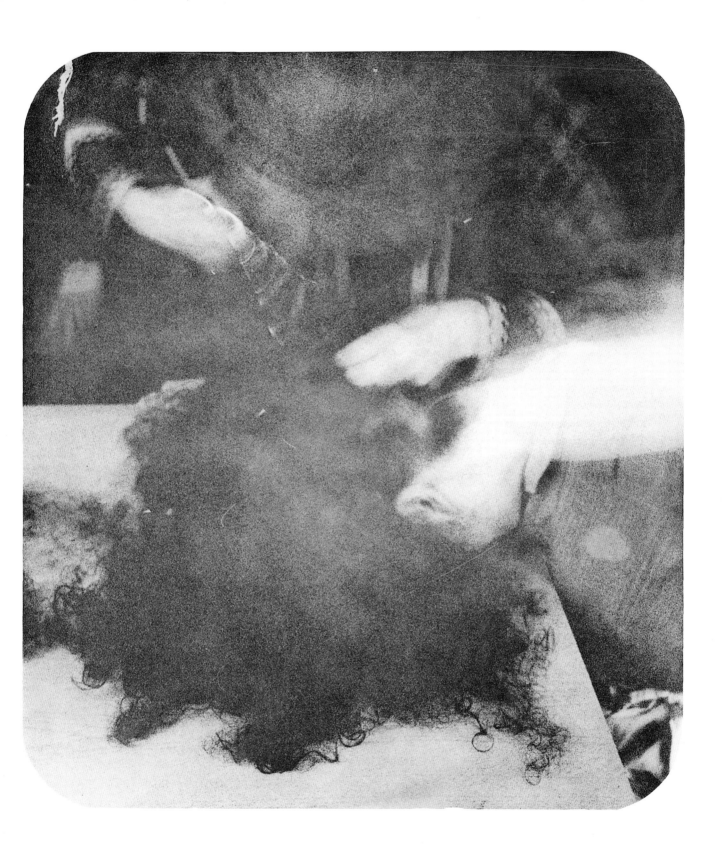

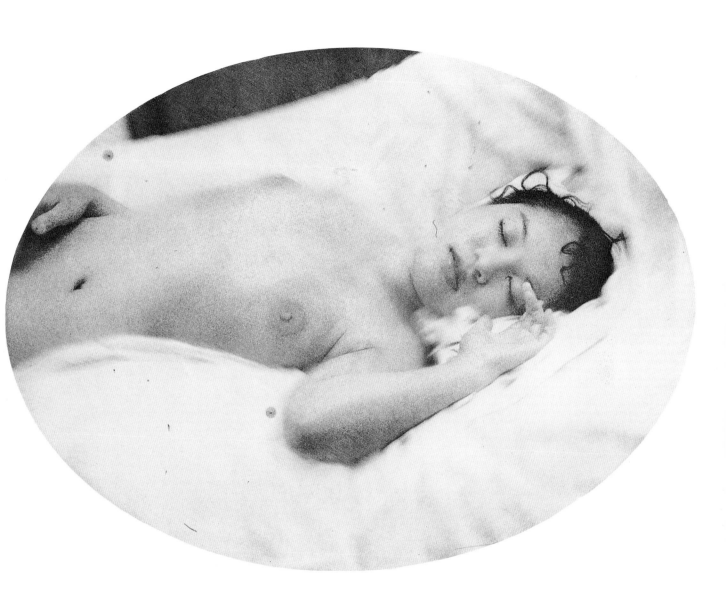

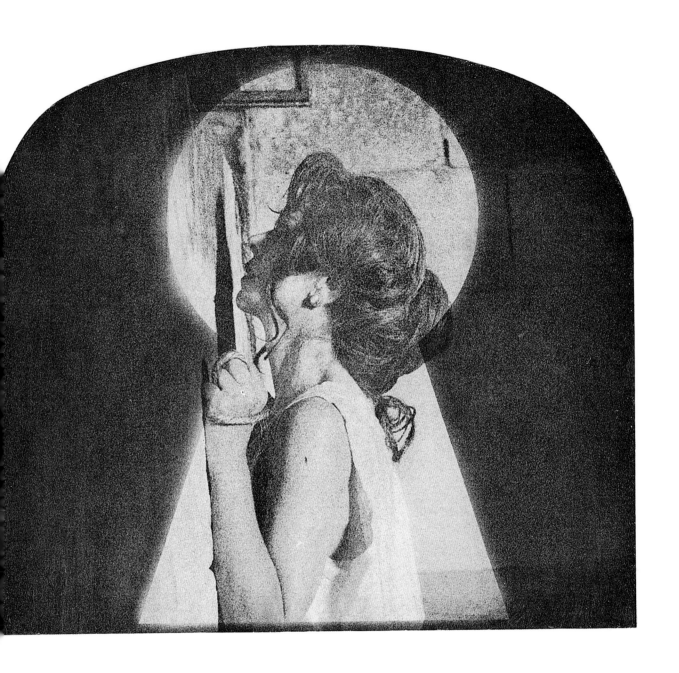

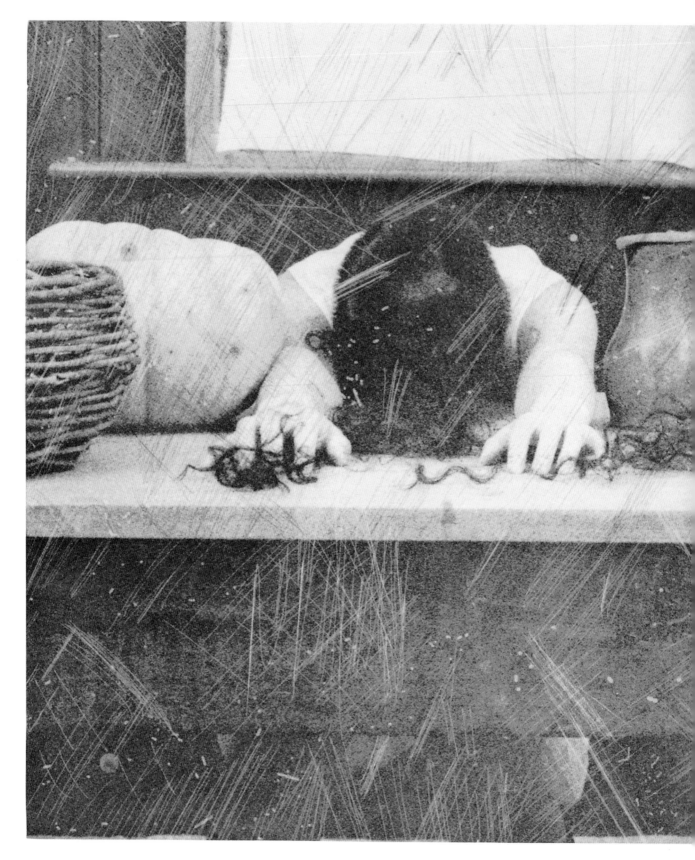

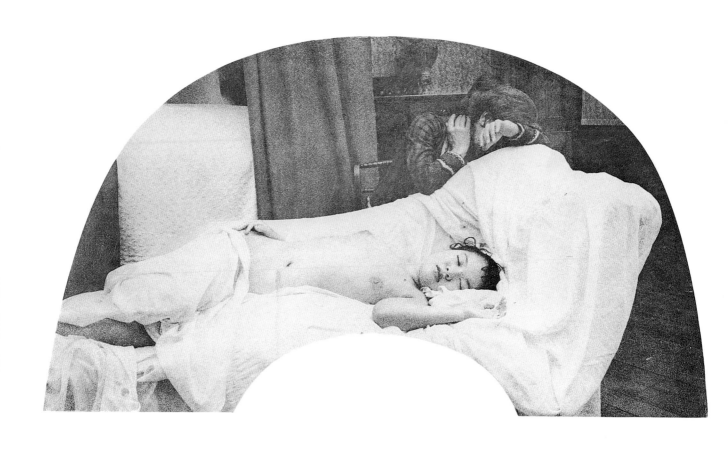

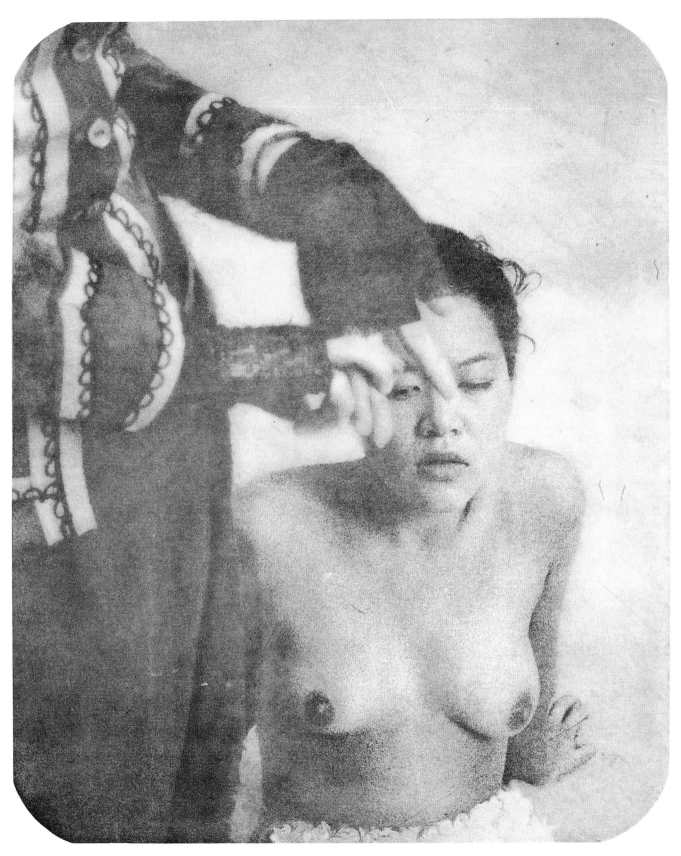

UP IN THE SKY

1997

Series of 25 offset prints
61 × 76 cm (image size), 72 × 102 cm (paper size)
edition of 60

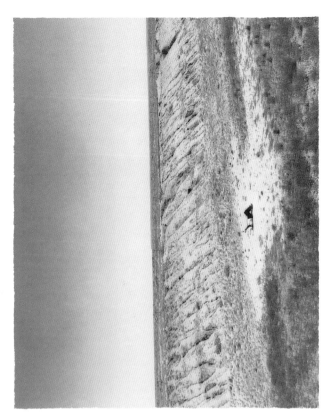

SCARRED FOR LIFE

1994

Series of nine offset prints
80 × 60 cm, edition of 50

Wizard of Oz, 1956

Birth Certificate, 1962

Charm Alone, 1965

Heart Attack, 1970

Doll Birth, 1972

Useless, 1974

Mother's Day, 1975

Job Hunt, 1976

Telecam Guys, 1977

Tracey Moffatt

The Wizard of Oz, 1956

He was playing Dorothy in the school's production of the *Wizard of Oz*.
His father got angry at him for getting dressed too early.

Birth Certificate, 1962 During the fight, her mother threw her birth certificate at her.
This is how she found out her real father's name.

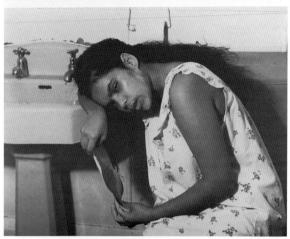

Tracey Moffatt

Tracey Moffatt

Charm Alone, 1965

His brother said, *'crooked nose and no chin –
you'll have to survive on charm alone'.*

Tracey Moffatt

Tracey Moffatt

Heart Attack, 1970 She glimpsed her father belting the
girl from down the street.
That day he died of a heart attack.

Doll Birth, 1972 His mother caught him giving birth to a doll.
He was banned from playing with the boy
next door again.

Tracey Moffatt

Useless, 1974
Her father's nickname for her was 'useless'.

Tracey Moffatt

Tracey Moffatt

Job Hunt, 1976
After three weeks he still couldn't find a job.
His mother said to him, 'maybe you're *not good enough*'.

Telecam Guys, 1977
Later, her sister said, 'the Telecam guys told me I was
far more more attractive and vivacious'.

Tracey Moffatt

SOMETHING MORE

1989

Series of six cibachrome and three black & white photographs
100 × 130 cm, edition of 30

BRISBANE 300

BEDEVIL

1993

90-minute film

NIGHT CRIES: A RURAL TRAGEDY

1990

17-minute film

Tracey
Moffatt

Stills from the documentary film by Jane Cole,
Up in the Sky: Tracey Moffatt in New York, 1999
(26 minutes)

AN INTERVIEW WITH TRACEY MOFFATT

BY

GERALD MATT

Deleuze and Parnet once said: 'Empiricists are not theoreticians, they are experimenters: they never interpret'. Do you see yourself as more of an 'experimenting artist'—within the meaning of the above quote—even though your works are based on detailed preparations and concepts?
The most interesting artists in history have always been experimenting artists. Most artists I know are such dissatisfied people, dissatisfied with everything so of course they must constantly be reinventing with their art. Perhaps this dissatisfaction is the reason that they are artists in the first place—I know it is with me.

Although I make careful detailed preparations before I work in my films and photography one must always be open to elements of surprise that do surface. I can have an original idea for an image and plan it out but the final outcome can be something different. My final image of choice can have a slightly different mood and feel. Most of the time it is better.

In an interview, you called yourself an 'image-maker'. The pictures you make are cinematographic or photographic, using media that reproduce reality. However, your pictures are characterised by an alienation of reality, partly by exaggeration, by surreality. When referring to your representations of nature, you like using the expression 'landscape of imagination'. In interviews and texts, reference is made to aboriginal art, dreams, some genres of film or painting in this context. What is the relation between realistic and fictitious means, especially when it comes to getting messages across?
I think all my imagery comes from my subconscious, from dreams. I am not talking about when I dream at night (these are far too weird and sick) but the dreams I have

when I am awake. We can dream with our eyes open. This is why I have been hesitant to be written about as a social commentator. I think my work is very dream-like.

The *Up in the Sky* pictures look a little like photo documentary, but there is still a surreal quality. Some of the images are in fact what I saw and photographed but most are staged up, set up. I like that people can't tell which is which, I like that there is an 'in-betweenness' about them.

In the *Guapa* pictures the women roller derby queens are obviously shot in a studio. I wanted it to feel like a nowhere space. I like that the images lack a time frame—they're just hanging there.

What are the most significant sources you tap into when creating the fictitious/artificial part of your pictures?
I like to create my version of reality, the work comes from me, what I know. Things I have seen and experienced, and things I think I have seen and experienced. Maybe it's just an exaggerated version of my reality. Sources of inspiration come from everywhere, from the beautiful formal quality of 1960's Japanese cinema—films such as Kabayoshi's *Kwaidan* (1964). This was a film of four ghost stories shot entirely in a studio with artificial sets—Kabayoshi apparently even painted the sky backdrop himself.

But then I can look at trash-TV—this is what I grew up with. I didn't grow up with 'high-culture', so for me as far as visual went, it was television. I am from a working class background, and I was only accessing what was available. But thank god I also read a lot—everything from Charles Dickens and the Brontés to comic books (which I would beat my brother up for) to soft porn (which I would take to school to be popular with).

Were there any specific films important for your work—e.g. the bizarre Australian cinema classic

Charles Chauvel's *Jedda* from 1955? And what about horror movies?

Jedda was an overblown melodramatic and I think racist Australian film made in the style of a Hollywood western. It was about an Aboriginal girl taken from her tribe and raised by a family as a white girl on a desert cattle property. I cannot bring myself to say that *Jedda* was an 'important' film, but I certainly liked the look of it. I recreated the interior set of the cattle property's main house and put it into my own short film *Night Cries*.

Most of all I suppose it is the visual element in certain cinema that is inspiring me. But feel and mood often come from literature, and in particular southern American writers such as Tennessee Williams, Truman Capote and the great Carson McCullers—a woman writer who I believe originally inspired Truman Capote. These writings always remind me of where I come from—the North of Australia, the sub-tropics. In a sense a holiday paradise—the heat, the joy but also the terrible mood of fear and racism. This mood is evident in my *Something More* photo series.

As for horror film I think nothing has ever matched Hollywood's *The Exorcist*. It's the scariest film ever made. I like a lot of Hollywood movies, I like the Italian American directors like Martin Scorsese, I like *Terminator II* and the *Mad Max* trilogy—it is the big spectacle that appeals.

But I always have a weakness for anything European—made before 1970 and in black and white like the dream films of Jean Cocteau. What an artist he was! His skill in changing between the different media—he made films, he wrote plays and designed for the theatre and what about his beautiful drawings. One of his famous quotes is: 'When the pillow is warm you must turn it over' … For me he is the artist's artist.

What about painting, as an artistic language, also in respect of its flexibility in creation?

You know when it comes down to it I wish I was a painter. There isn't anything greater and nothing hypnotises like painting. Nothing fascinates more than what the human hand can do. I think for 99 per cent of people to this day photography and film is a foreign media. It is technical, expensive and most people don't get the chance to try it. From an early age, all of us in every culture in the world have been handed a pencil, a brush and some paper. From the first day of school we are made to make our mark but very soon most of us discover to our own horror that we can't do it—except for Johnny in the next row. Does Johnny grow up to become an artist? Very rarely.

So for most of us this must be the first tragic inadequate thing we find out about ourselves—that we can't

move paint around. I know that I can't move paint around, you can look at my awful storyboards to see this—so I moved into other areas. Perhaps my work is all about painting—sometimes writers describe my 'palette'. This delights me.

I would like to mention Georgia O'Keeffe. I first came across her in art school, there was a revival of her in the early eighties. The interesting thing about her was that she was completely American and that she wasn't looking a real lot to Europe for her sources.

Susan Sontag once said: 'Only that which narrates can make us understand.' Your films and photo series also often have a narrative element. How important is the narrative for your work—e.g. from the angle of linking real and artificial components? Does it serve to enhance understanding, the way Sontag said?

My work is full of emotion and drama, you can get to that drama by using a narrative, and my narratives are usually very simple, but I twist it. In the *Up in the Sky* pictures there is a story line, but the hanging order of the pictures can change it around. There isn't a traditional beginning, middle and end. You can be in the present and shift to the past and come back to the present—it's playing with time and space. As for Sontag's saying that 'only what narrates can make us understand'—unfortunately in the case of what I do and the reactions I've had from a lot of people—my twisted narratives only serve to *baffle!*

Would you link the historically or culturally significant traditions you use in your works (e.g. 'ghost-stories' of Aborigines or the cycle of Irish legends in *beDevil*) with the notion of mythology? How would you define this notion, which you actually do not use yourself as far as I know, and how does it relate to your work?

It is a personal mythology that I use. I wouldn't say that I was drawing on Aboriginal legends, stories because I think that it is too easy and I actually think that I don't have a right to do it. My images are so personal that a lot of time they embarrass me. I'm always saying: 'Oh my God, don't make me watch *Night Cries* again!'

For me the film is deep and it probably has something to do with my relationship with my mother—the love, the hate. I made this film at a time when I had these feelings but now I don't have them any more. Must be a Freudian thing when artists say that their work 'repulses them'. Look at Woody Allen, he can't stand to look at his films so don't make me look at mine.

'Multi-cultural' is a buzzword frequently applied to your work. Occasionally, I believe I can detect ironic elements when you deal with ethno-social themes, expressed e.g. in the idea of trading roles or plays on clichés (as in *Nice Coloured Girls*). Is there a political intention behind your work? How do the respective ethnic communities react to your way of representation?

Within all my work I want to create a world, a general world. Australia is a very multi-cultural nation and this has certainly influenced my work. So I don't want to make some grand statement on race—it isn't about wanting to be politically correct, perhaps it's about always striving for an 'international' look to my work.

I have made political films, once in 1983 I worked on a documentary about an Aboriginal land rights protest which was both exhilarating and a nightmare. Some members of the group or rather the 'collective' I made it with didn't agree with the film so they destroyed it (literally with scissors—on the night of the film's premier they chopped up nine months of hard work) and it was never seen.

This incident turned me off making political films. But the irony is, and we all know this today that these important well made documentaries about issues like Indigenous land rights and the nuclear disarmament and the environment really did help to reveal things—educate the public and change the world.

I want to say that if people want to read my art that I'm making now from a political perspective then they are welcome. I just get a little exasperated because this reading usually comes from the 'left' and they are most of the time ignoring how I strive for poetry and make statements about the human condition—they can't see that I'm trying to play with form and be inventive.

I think that the fact that I'm trying for a 'universal' quality, not just 'black Australian' is the reason why my work is getting attention. But try telling this to some writers ….

The artificial part of your work also includes the formal aspect of fabrication, staging, choreography in your pictures. This is true of many of your films and photo series. Moreover, some critics think that your photo series have 'still photography' qualities. This is corroborated by a look at your storyboards.

I have never just produced a single photograph and tried to make it stand alone as an artistic statement. Though of course art collectors have bought single images from my series—so perhaps certain pictures do appeal by them-

selves. For me it is the narrative. It is difficult for me to say anything in one single image. With working in a photographic serial I can expand one idea—give it further possibilities. It makes photography close to film in its possibilities.

Every photo series changes completely in look—colour or no colour—glossy or matt—big or small. I don't believe that I have an identifiable style, because I don't do the same thing twice. I don't think one can readily look at my pictures and say 'oh yes, that's a Tracey Moffatt'. Not in the way you can say this with a Robert Mapplethorpe print. When I first saw a Mapplethorpe picture I couldn't get over the shocking deadly precision in them—they were like ice. Photography never looked like that before him—now it's commonplace, it's everywhere—in advertising especially.

With the *Scarred for Life* photo series I have again changed the format. I have integrated rather ordinary washed out colour compositions with text describing the scene. I was inspired by looking at 1960s American *Life* magazine layouts. A kind of snapshot photography—very everyday moments based on real life tragic funny childhood stories of my friends and myself. I felt that this was the only way to keep power in the image—to be ordinary, it does resonate. People remember the little boy giving birth to the doll. I could have shot this in a more clever dramatic way but in the end it had to be like a scene one would see as they passed and glanced in the living room door. In the case of this picture it is the mean mother's point of view. Also as well at the time I made this work I had no money—it was a purely practical thing to produce something low key and inexpensive.

Now in 1998 I have more money and I'm making an elaborate photo series based on historical erotic texts. Please don't ask me to say more on this—I believe it is bad luck to talk an idea up too much before you execute it. Just shut the hell up and do it, is my motto—words are cheap!

What are the specific qualities film and photography have for you (e.g. as regards to immobility/ movement, and reception)? How much leeway is there for e.g. spontaneity in your photographs and films? Where do you place yourself?

I love both film and photography. I don't want to create a division. My relationship to film and photography has to do with, as I mentioned previously, such things as money. It is a long time in-between film projects—film costs so much money and you have to find this money. So in the meantime I'm going crazy—my obsession to create makes me crabby.

Photography is much less expensive—less equipment needed, smaller teams to work with, etc. Photography is always a wonderful challenge, it is all about what one can pull off with a camera, it's the way you use a camera and then how you choose to print the images—so many possibilities it is mind boggling. Of course now with computer manipulations the possibilities make you exhausted even thinking about it.

I like the art world as well as opposed to the film world (though both can be just as pretentious). I've just gotten sick of being literally pushed around at those crowded loud international film festivals although I guess the Venice Biennale is not different! I like seeing things on white walls. The contemporary art world is light years ahead in ideas. So often it is much more rewarding intellectually for me to have 'exhibitions' as opposed to 'film screenings'. Let's face it, hardly anything (save a few things) inventive and stimulating and beautiful has been made in cinema past the date of 1977. I have a theory about this but won't go into it now. Don't start me off!

How do you relate to the traditions of photography and cinema?
I am constantly scanning old photography books and old films. There is no way that one can be an artist of substance without doing one's homework.

In your works you frequently appear as a performer (*Something More*, *Pet Thang*, *beDevil*, *Scarred for Life*). What is the part that autobiographical elements play for you, in the context of self-expression on the one hand, and in the engagement with more general social, cultural and political themes on the other.
It is often a technically practical thing to cast myself in my work. Often I can't find anyone else to do it—often as well as a money saving thing. It feels as natural for me to be in front of a camera as behind it.

In fact I have never analysed this—as I try not to with most things. When one is too academic it gets in the way of creation. I have no precise plans to appear in my future films or photographs. It's not like I'm Cindy Sherman (I do love her fat ugly wizard series from 1996). I like to direct and cast other people though this is always the hardest thing in the creation of my art—to find the right face. I go insane running after people I see on the street and often I get insulted!

Maybe the autobiographical aspects in my work have to do with using myself—probably it is as simple as this.

In an interview you once said you were a 'control freak'. You also direct your films, as you told

before. For your photo series you recruit professional teams, work in studios, with actors and props similar to movie production. You are scriptwriter, performer/ actress and director, all rolled into one. The fact that you fulfil such a multiplicity of functions indicates that you, as an avant-garde film-maker, have the greatest possible share in the work, but the massive expenditure involved in the production also points to commercial cinema.
Control freak? Yes! I do want everything my way—to begin with. One has to keep some sort of control. But I love teamwork nevertheless. If I didn't like to work with people I would be a painter—like my fantasy—alone in my studio with my brushes and canvasses and paint in my hair, with the answering machine on all the time. But I like communication—I think I can communicate well though I'm demanding.

I like to bring the best out of my collaborators. They are always throwing in their ideas—how can they not contribute? They are creative people whom I choose for a reason and I'm lucky to be working with them.

For example, for my film *Night Cries* I worked with a wonderful theatre designer, Stephen Curtis, who created a very hard, artificial desert landscape of the Australian outback. I initially wasn't so sure about it being so hard but I went with his interpretation of my script. Now of course I like what he did. When the film premiered at Cannes Film Festival—seven years ago—some critics thought I was influenced by Robert Wilson, the avant-garde American theatre director. At the time I was not familiar with Robert Wilson's work.

So I can either take my creative teams' ideas on board or not use them. But initially it is always Ms Moffatt's ideas and obsessions they are helping to put on the gallery wall or on the big screen.

None of them should complain because I always pay them well!

Is the boundary between avant-garde film and mainstream cinema of any importance to you? Could you imagine working in something like 'mainstream cinema' in the future?
I do want to make a mainstream film. I'm working on a film script now which I cry over because it is so hard to do. It will be as challenging as anything I've ever tried to pull off. As an artist you must face change. This also has to do with my energy—I always want to move onto the next thing. I think it is fine to switch between worlds like loving both trash and classical and obscure literature and going from Antonioni to Schwarzenegger.

But one of the main reasons is, as I regretfully rocket towards 40 … is that I want to finally make some money.

BIOGRAPHY & BIBLIOGRAPHY

Tracey Moffatt
Born 1960, Brisbane
Lives and works in Sydney and New York

SELECTED SOLO EXHIBITIONS

2000
Laudanum, Yerba Buena Center, San Francisco
1999
Tracey Moffatt, Institute of Modern Art, Brisbane, and touring
    through Northern Asia
Tracey Moffatt, Galerie Laage—Saloman, Paris, France; Freiburger
    Kunsverin, Freiberg, Germany; Centre National de la Photogra-
    phie, Paris, France; Galerie Schneider, Karlruhe, Germany
Tracey Moffatt, Neueer Berliner Kunstverien, Berlin, Germany
Laudanum, Rupertinum, Salzberg, Austria
Tracey Moffatt, Centro Galego de Arte Contemporain, Santiago de
    Compostela, Spain
Tracey Moffatt, Ulmer Museum, Ulm, Germany
Tracey Moffatt, Six Freidrich, Lisa Ungar Gallery, Münich, Germany
Tracey Moffatt, Torch Gallery, Amsterdam, The Netherlands
Laudanum, Roslyn Oxley9 Gallery, Sydney; LA Galerie, Frankfurt,
    Germany
Laudanum, Paul Morris Gallery, New York, USA
Laudanum, Victoria Miro Gallery, London, UK
Tracey Moffatt, Lawing Gallery, Houston, USA
Tracey Moffatt, Up in the Sky, Le Case D'Arte, Milan, Italy
Tracey Moffatt, Galeria Helgade Alvear, Madrid, Spain
Tracey Moffatt, Fundacío 'la Caixa', Sala San Juan, Barcelona,
    Spain; *Free-Falling*, ICA, Boston, USA; Rena Bransten Gallery,
    San Francisco, USA; Le Case D'Arte, Milano, Italy; Curtin Uni-
    versity Gallery, Perth
1998
Tracey Moffatt, Galleri Larsen, Stockholm, Sweden
Tracey Moffatt, Arnolfini, Bristol, UK
Free-Falling, The Renaissance Society, Chicago, USA

Up in the Sky, Roslyn Oxley9 Gallery, Sydney
Tracey Moffatt, Le Case D'Arte, Milano, Italy; Victoria Miro Gallery,
    London, UK; Curtin University, Perth; L.A. Galerie, Frankfurt,
    Germany; Kunsthalle Vienna, Vienna, Austria; Wurttembergis-
    cher Kunstverein, Stuttgart, Germany; Il Ponte
    Contamporanea, Rome, Italy; AR/GE KUNST Galerie Museum,
    Bozen/Bolzano, Italy; Galleri Faurschou, Copenhagen, Den-
    mark; Voralberger Kunstverein, Bregenz, Austria; Australian
    Centre for Contemporary Art, Melbourne; Fundació, 'la Caiza',
    Barcelona, Spain
1997
Free-Falling, Dia Center for the Arts, New York, USA
Tracey Moffatt, L.A. Galerie, Frankfurt, Germany; Galerie Andreas
    Weiss, Berlin, Germany; Galleri Faurschou, Copenhagen,
    Denmark; Fond Régional d'Art Contemporain, Dijon, France;
    Casino Luxembourg, Luxembourg, Belgium
Tracey Moffatt, Films, Musée d'Art Contemporain, Lyon, France
1995
Guapa (Goodlooking), Karyn Lovegrove Gallery, Melbourne; Mori
    Gallery, Sydney
Short Takes, ArtPace, San Antonio, Texas, USA
1994
Scarred for Life, Karyn Lovegrove Gallery, Melbourne
1992
Pet Thang, Mori Gallery, Sydney; Centre of Contemporary Arts,
    Glasgow, Scotland
1989
Something More, Australian Centre for Photography, Sydney,
    (toured through regional galleries in Australia)
1988
Shades of Light, National Gallery of Australia, Canberra
1987
Art and Aboriginality, Aspex Gallery, Portsmouth, UK
1986
Aboriginal and Islander Photographs, Aboriginal Artists Gallery,
    Sydney

SELECTED GROUP EXHIBITIONS

1999

Rosa für Jungs, Weiß für Mädchen, Neue Gesellschaft für bildende Kunst, Berlin, Germany

100 Meisterwerke aus Malerie, Fotografie, Skulptur and Intallationskunst, Lehmbachhaus, Münich, Germany: touring to Von der Heydt Museum, Wuppertal, Germany and Kunstsammlung Bötcherstraße, Bremen, Germany

Signature Works, Australian Centre for Photography, Sydney

1998

Museum van Hedendaagse Kunst Gent, Gent, Belgium

Family Viewing, Musuem of Contemporary Art, Los Angeles, USA

Portraits, Paul Morris Gallery, New York, USA

Echolot, Museum Fridericianum, Kassel, Germany

Foto Triennale Esslingen, Esslingen, Germany

Musée Départemental d'Art Contemporain, Rochechouart, France

'Die Nerven enden an den Fingerspitzen', Die Sammlungen Wilhelm Schürmann, Kunsthaus Hamburg, Germany

National Museum for Photography, Coppenhagen, Denmark

Presumed Innocence, Anderson Gallery, Richmond, USA

Strange days—Guiness Contemporary Art Exhibition, Art Gallery of NSW, Sydney

1997

Site Santa Fe, Santa Fe, New Mexico, USA

On Dialogue. Zeitgenössische australische Kunst, Haus am Waldsee, Berlin, Germany

Biennale di Venezia, Venice, Italy

Mathew Marks Gallery, New York, USA; Anthony Reynolds Gallery, London, UK; Roslyn Oxley9 Gallery, Sydney

Printemps de Cahors, Paris, France

'steierischer herbst 97', Graz, Austria

'Campo 6', The Spiral Village, Bonnefanten Museum, Maastricht, The Netherlands

Subject to Representation, Gallery 101, Ottawa, Canada

1996

Fundacão Bienal de São Paulo, São Paulo, Brazil

'Campo 6', The Spiral Village, Museo d'Arte Moderna, Torino, Italy

Jurassic Technologies Revenant, 10th Biennale of Sydney, Sydney

Prospect 96, Schirn Kunsthalle, Frankfurt, Germany

1995

Antipodean Currents, Guggenheim Museum (Soho), New York, USA

Familiar Places, ICA, Boston, USA

'95 Kwangju Biennale, Kwangju, Korea

New Works 95.2, ArtPace, San Antonio, Texas, USA

Perspecta 95, Art Gallery of NSW, Sydney

1994

Antipodean Currents, The Kennedy Center, Washington, USA

Power Works, Govett Brewster Gallery, New Plymouth, New Zealand

Eidetic Experiences, toured through regional galleries in Qld

1993

The Boundary Rider, 9th Biennale of Sydney, Art Gallery of NSW, Sydney

FILM & VIDEO (WRITER/DIRECTOR)

Lip, 10-minute experimental video (collaboration with Gary Hillberg), 1999

Heaven, 28-minute video (commission Dia Center for the Arts, New York, USA), 1997

My Island Home, music video (Christine Anu), 1995

Let My Children Be, music video (Ruby Hunter), 1994

The Messenger, music video (INXS), 1993

beDevil, 90-minute feature drama (Official Selection Cannes 1993), 1993

Night Cries—A Rural Tragedy, 17-minute drama (O.S.C. 1990), 1989

It's Up to You, 9-minute health video

Moodeitj Yorgas, 22-minute documentary, 1988

A Change of Face, 3 part documentary SBS TV (co-director), 1988

Watch Out, 5-minute dance video, Flim Australia, 1987

Nice Coloured Girls, 16-minute experimental film, 1987

The Rainbow Serpent, documentary series SBS TV (stills photography), 1985

PHOTOGRAPHY COLLECTIONS

MOCA, Los Angeles • Refco, Inc, Chicago • Musee for Santidskunst, Oslo • Museum of Contemporary Photography, Tokyo • DG Bank, Frankfurt • Museum Folkwang, Essen • Collection of Mr & Mrs Felten, Münich • Collection of Mr Kunne, Hannover • Lousiana Museum of Contemporary Art, Humblebaek • Linda Pace Collection, San Antonio • Australian National Gallery, Canberra • Art Gallery of New South Wales, Sydney • National Gallery of Victoria, Melbourne • Museum of Contemporary Art, Sydney • Flinders University, Adelaide • Queensland Art Gallery, Brisbane • Griffith University, Brisbane • Monash University, Melbourne • Art Gallery of South Australia, Adelaide • National Library, Canberra • Tasmanian State Institute of Technology, Hobart • Albury Regional Art Gallery, Albury • BP Australia, Melbourne • Steve Vizard Foundation, Melbourne • Art Gallery of Western Australia, Perth • Curtin University, Perth • NRMA Collection, Sydney

FILM & VIDEO COLLECTIONS

New York Public Library, New York • National Library, Canberra • State Film and Video Library, Adelaide • Curtin University, Perth • West Australian Institute of Technology, Perth • Griffith University, Brisbane • Macquarie University, Sydney • University of Technology, Sydney • Sydney University, Sydney • State Film Centre, Melbourne • West Australian Film Centre, Perth • Institute of Aboriginal Studies, ANU, Canberra

FILM & VIDEO DISTRIBUTORS

Roin Films, Canberra • Southern Star, Sydney • Australian Film Institute, Melbourne • Women Make Movies, New York, USA • Circles, London, UK • Women in Focus, Vancouver, Canada

SELECTED BIBLIOGRAPHY

Martin Hentschel, Gerald Matt (eds), *Tracey Moffatt*, exh.cat. Kunsthalle Wien, Vienna, Austria; Württembergischer, Kunstverein Stuttgart, Germany; AR/GE KUNST, Bozen, Italy; Vorarlberger Kunstverein, Bregenz, Austria, 1998

Wayne Tunnicliffe (ed.), 'Tracey Moffatt', in: *Strange Days*, exh.cat. Art Gallery of NSW, Sydney, 1998

Susan Lowish, 'Free-falling', in: *Flash*, Centre for Contemporary Photography, Melbourne, November 1998

Adrian Martin, 'Ewa Lajer-Burcharth',in: *Parkett*, Zurich, Switzerland, no.53, 1998

Jennifer Higgie, 'Tracey Moffatt—Victoria Miro',in: *Frieze*, London, UK, no. 40, May 1998

Ludovica Pratesi, 'Turn-of-the-century reflections: Six chapters on art and jeans' in: *Art energie: Art in Jeans*, exh.cat. Florence, Italy, 1998

Rene Block (ed), *Escholot*, exh.cat. Museum Fridericianum, Kassel, Germany, 1998

Lynne Cooke, *Tracey Moffatt: Free-falling*, exh.cat. Dia Center for the Arts, New York, USA, 1997

Fundacao Bienal de São Paulo, exh.cat. São Paulo, Brazil, 1997

Francesco Bonami (ed.), *'Campo 6', The spiral village*, exh.cat. Museo d'Arte Moderna, Torino, Italy, 1996

Julia Robinson, *Antipodean currents*, exh.cat. Guggenheim Museum, Soho, New York, USA, July 1995

Frances Colpitt (ed.), 'Tracey Moffatt—Guapa (Goodlooking)', exh.cat. *New works show*, ArtPace, San Antonio, USA, 1995

Gael Newton, Tracey Moffatt (eds), *Tracey Moffatt: Fever pitch*, Piper Press, Sydney, 1995

Gael Newton, 'Tracey Moffatt', exh.cat. *Australian Perspecta 95*, Art Gallery of NSW, Sydney, 1995

Tait Brady, 'beDevil', exh.cat. *Melbourne film festival 1993*, Melbourne 1993

Jacques Delaruelle, 'On the verge of saying nothing', exh.cat. *Visual arts programme, Adelaide festival 1993*, Adelaide, 1993

Terence Maloon, *From the empire's end: Nine Australian photographers*, exh.cat. Circulo de Bellas Artes, Madrid,Spain; The Works Gallery, University of NSW, Sydney, 1990

Isobel Crombie, Sandra Byron (eds), *Twenty contemporary Australian photographers*, exh.cat. National Gallery of Australia, Canberra, 1990

Anne Marie Willis, in: *Picturing Australia: A history of photography*, Angus & Robertson, Sydney, 1989

Gael Newton, *Shades of light: Photography and Australia,* exh.cat. Australian National Gallery, Canberra, 1988

Helen Ennis, *Australian photography: The 1980's*, exh.cat. Australian National Gallery, Canberra, 1988